I LOVE YOU

My Happy Heart

MELODY CARLSON

ILLUSTRATED BY Jim Osborn

BROADMAN &HOLMAN PUBLISHERS

Nashville, Tennessee

Dedicated to the Collman grandkids,
Kiwani, Bonnie, Cody, Sophia, Hannah, and Wyatt.
Best Blessings!
Melody

Text copyright 2000 by Melody Carlson

Illustration copyright © 2000 by Jim Osborn

Published in 2000 by Broadman & Holman Publishers

Nashville, Tennessee

Design and layout by Paul T. Gant Art & Design.

A catalog record for this book is available

from the Library of Congress.

Do you know why
my heart's happy?
Do you know what
makes me smile?
I'd really like to tell you,
But it might take
just a while.

It's not that it's a secret,
Or something hard to know.
It's just that it is special,
But it's something I can show.

First I do some thinking.
Sometimes I close my eyes.
I think of all my favorite friends—
From pets to girls to guys.

I think of how I love them,
And how they warm my heart.
And when I want to tell them.
I know just where to start.

First I find
my crayons,
Some paper,
scissors, paste.
I draw a great,
big happy heart.
My message,
carefully placed!

Then I do
some coloring,
I do some
cutting too.
I paste and fold
and cut some more.
Still only
halfway through.

Next will come
the fun part,
When I choose
who I will pick,
To give my
happy letter to.
But choosing
is a trick.

I put it in
my pocket.
And I hurry
on my way,
To see the
people that I love,
Who will I
pick today?

I head on down
the hallway,
Spying Jenny
in her bed.
I stop and make
weird faces,
Then I stroke her
fuzzy head.

I tell her that
I love her...
For a baby,
she's okay.
But if she had
my letter,
She'd just
eat it anyway.

Next I see
my Daddy,
He's almost
out the door.
I run and yell,
"I love you!"
And he sweeps
me off the floor.

He tells me
to mind Mommy.
And that he
loves me too.
I think about
my letter and,
I'm not sure
what I'll do.

I hold onto
my letter,
As I sit on
our front porch.
Along comes
our cat Henry,
His tail held
like a torch.

His coat is warm
and furry.
As he purrs
into my ear.
I whisper that
I love him,
Then it's
Mommy's
voice, I hear.

"It's time to eat
your breakfast,"
Mommy tells me
with a smile.
And I think
about my letter,
But I guess
I'll wait a while.

Still, I say I love her,
And I think that
she's the best.
Then I pray
and ask God
For my pancakes
to be blessed.

With my letter
in my pocket.
I cross the school
playground.
I see so many,
many friends,
All running
all around.

There's Jamie and
there's Kelly,
There's Cassandra
and there's Paul.
But how can I
pick only one?
Of course,
I love them all!

And then when
school is over,
"See you later,"
calls Miss Crew.
I see her smile
and then I know
How much
I love her too!

I reach into
my pocket
And I almost
take it out—
Instead I grin
and wave to her,
"See you later, too!"
I shout.

Waiting by a
blue car,
I quickly
spot Aunt Kate.
She always picks
me up from school,
And she is
never late!

Then I realize
how I love her,
As she opens
the car door.
I pat my pocket
and I think,
Is she who
my card's for?

But still I
have my letter,
When she drops
me off at home.
And then I see
my neighbor,
The one who
lives alone.

I pick some
yellow flowers,
And I run
to say hello.
I give him a big,
friendly hug.
And then
I turn to go.

Then just a
little later,
Right at half
past three,
Grandpa comes
to my house,
He comes
to visit me!

We take a
walk together,
And he gives
my hand a squeeze.
I think about
my letter,
I think how
he'd be pleased.

At night Dad says,
"It's time for bed." And
my whole
day's been spent,
But my letter with
the happy heart,
Still has not
been sent!

The edges are
all rumpled,
And the paper's
turning gray.
The crayon on
the front is smeared.
I never
gave it away!

My pajamas on,
it's time to kneel,
Before my bed
and pray.
"I thank you, God,
for those I love,
And thanks for
this good day!"

"I made this card,
though it's not much,
It's rumpled
and it's small.
But, God, I give
my heart to you.
For I love you
best of all!"

"Thank you that
you fill my heart,
With all the
love you do,
I love you, God,
I always will—
My heart belongs to you!"